What Makes Everything Go?
An energy primer

Written and Illustrated

by

Michael Elsohn Ross

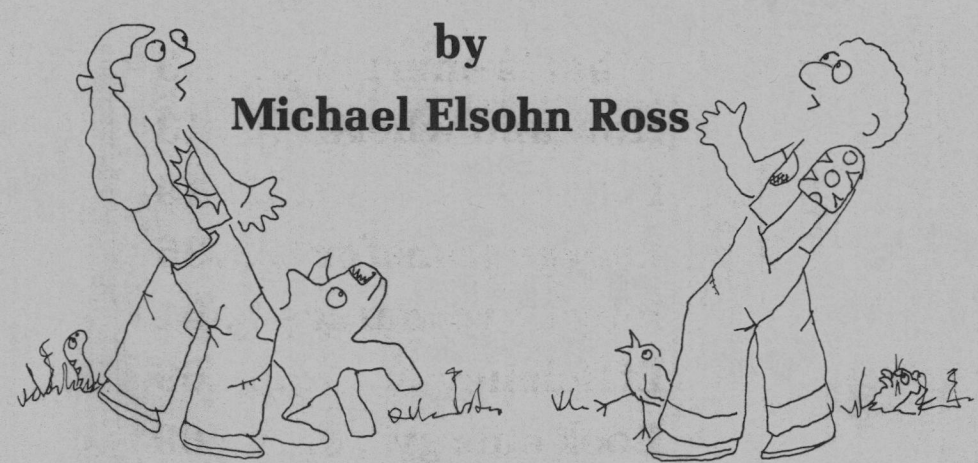

Published by

Yosemite Association

© 1979

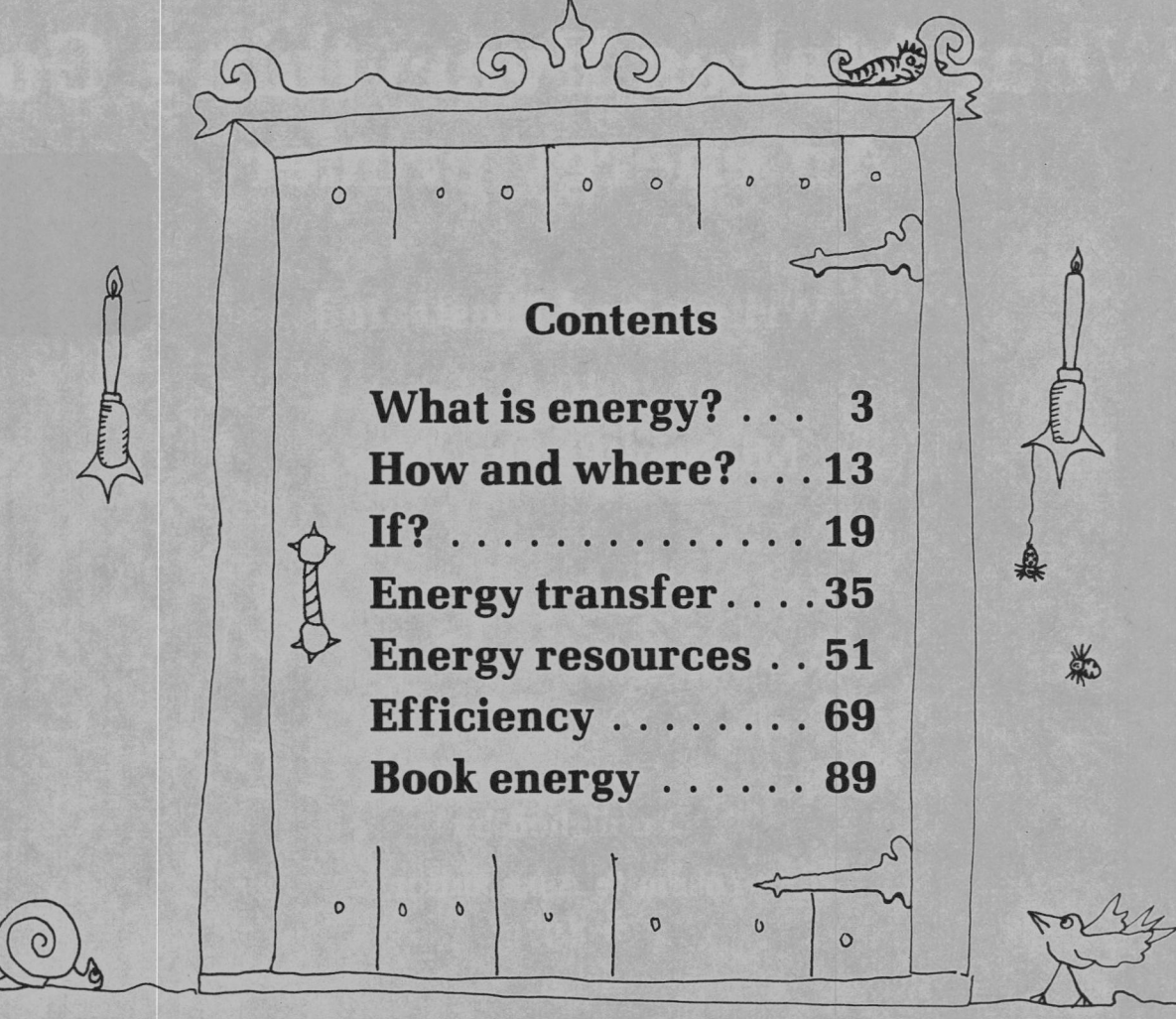

Contents

What is energy? ... 3
How and where? ... 13
If? ... 19
Energy transfer ... 35
Energy resources ... 51
Efficiency ... 69
Book energy ... 89

What is energy?

Do you remember what cycles are? **Yes, they are something that go around.**

This book is about the thing that makes cycles go.

What makes cycles go?

Energy!   **What is energy?**

Energy is what makes things change. **Does it make me grow?**

Energy makes kids grow.

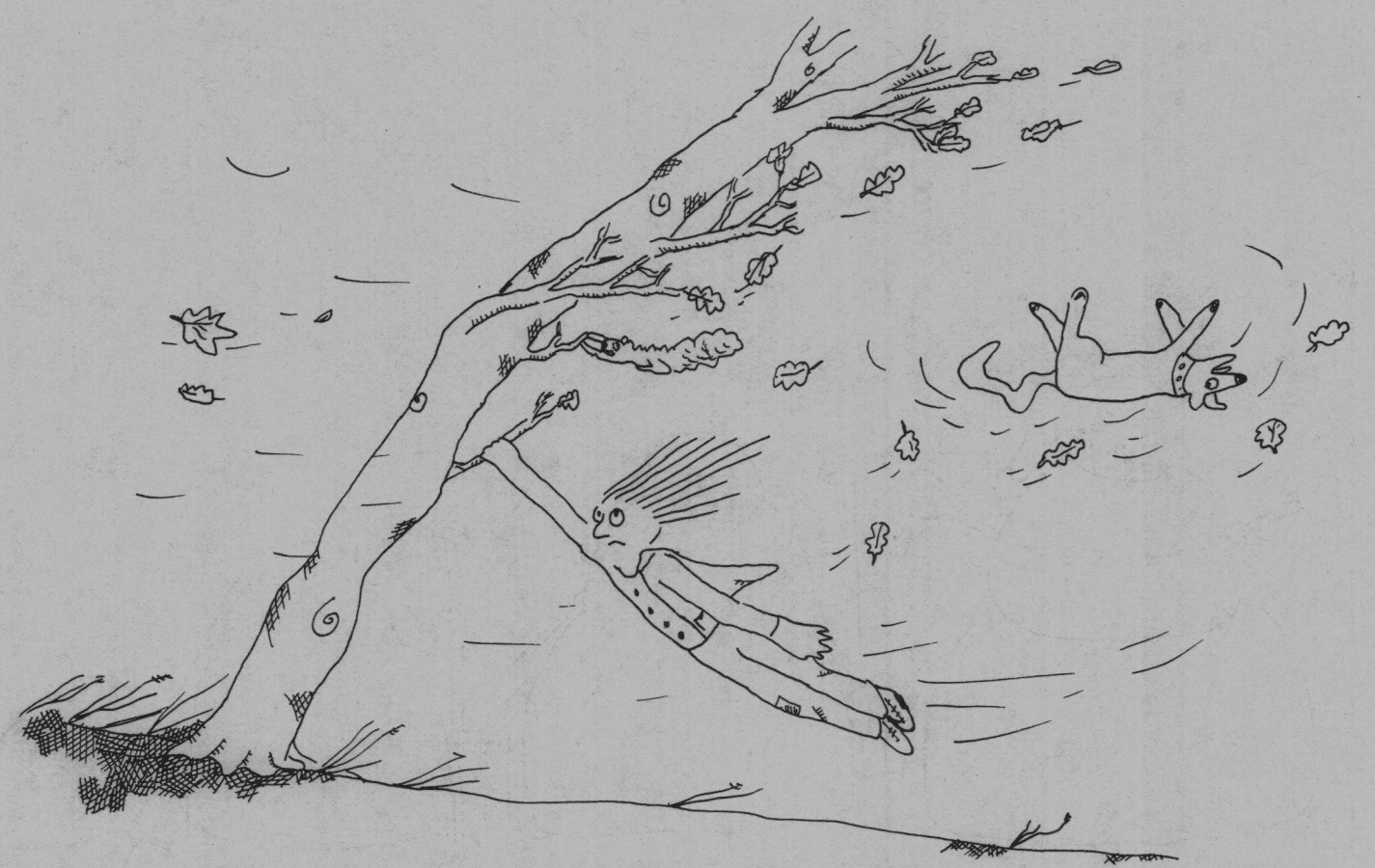

It makes the wind blow.

It melts snow.

It makes stars glow.

Energy makes everything go.

How and where?

Energy makes cycles go but it does not go in circles. **How does it go?**

In a straight line.

But WHERE does it go?

Energy goes from order.

to disorder.

IF

If you eat lunch

and then climb or lift heavy things,

you will change some of the food energy into heat.

Can you take that heat and change it back to food?

If you build a fire in your fireplace,

the burning logs will change to ashes, smoke and heat.

Can you take that heat, smoke and ash and change it back to wood?

If you use gas to make a car go,

the gas will change to smoke and heat.

Can you take that smoke and heat and change it back to gas?

Why?

Because energy doesn't go in circles!

ENERGY TRANSFER

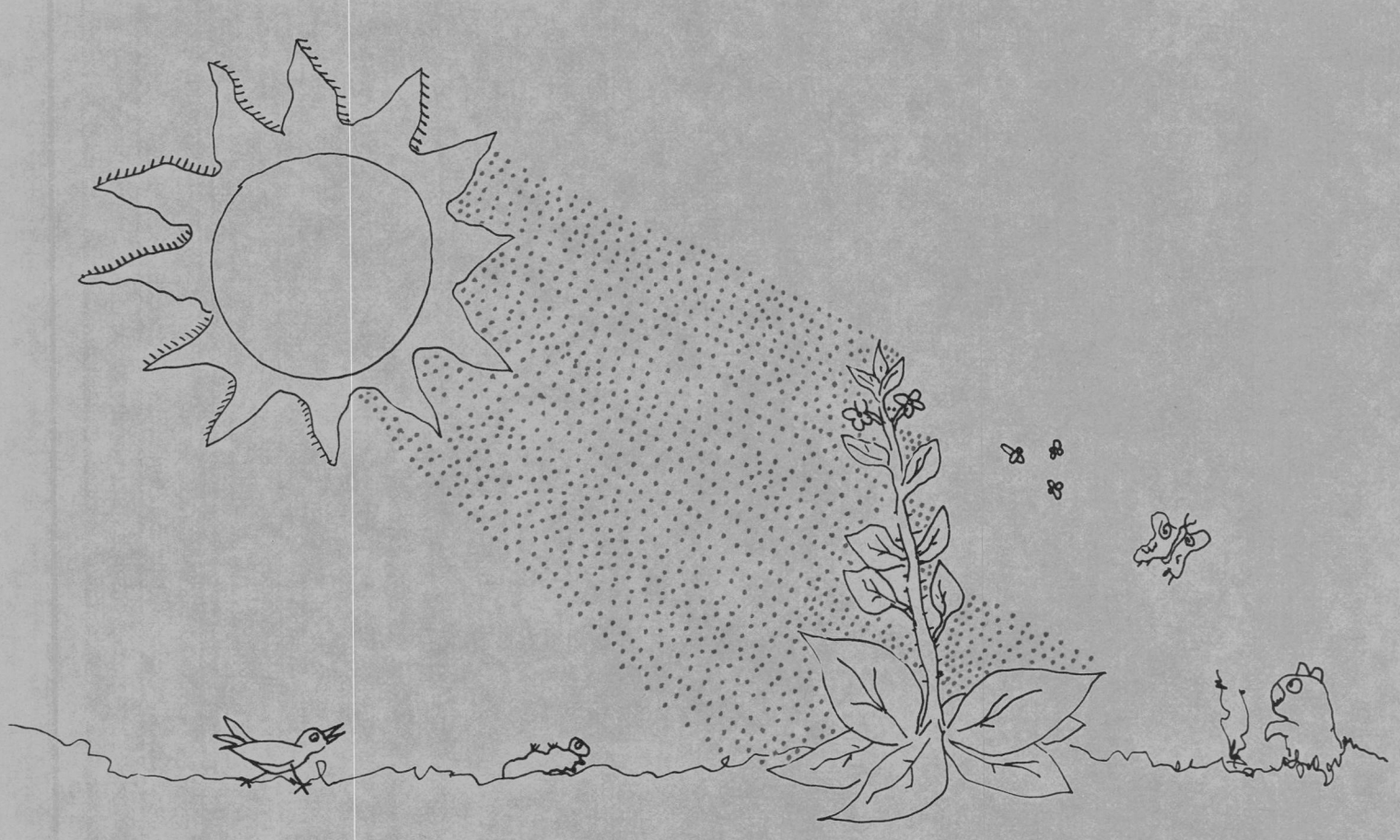

One day the sun sent 1,000 bits of energy to a plant.

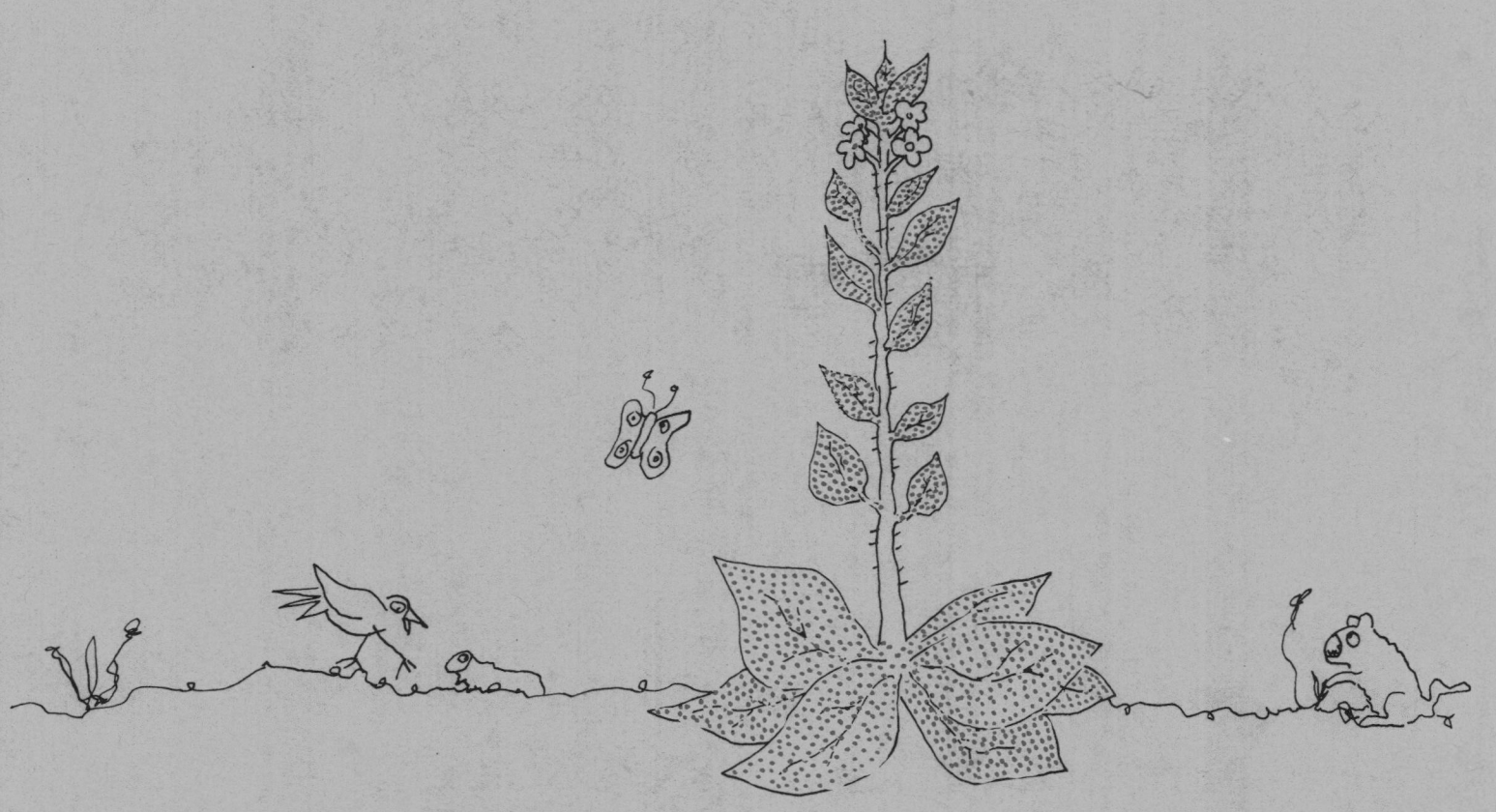

The plant used the bits of sun energy to help it grow.

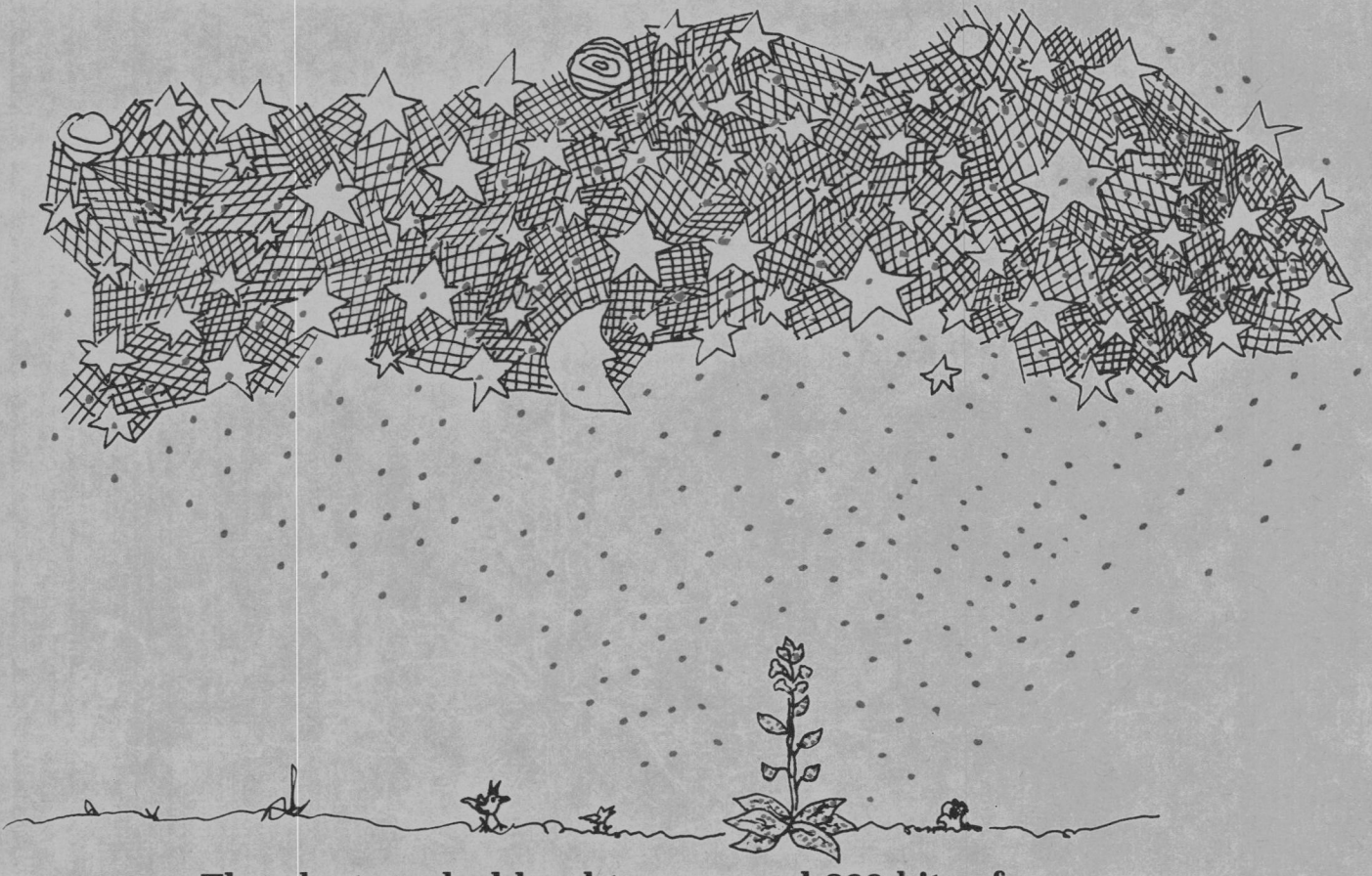

The plant worked hard to grow and 900 bits of sun energy changed to heat. The heat just floated away.

Only 100 bits stayed in the plant.

A spiny plant eater came and ate the plant.

It got the 100 bits of sun energy.

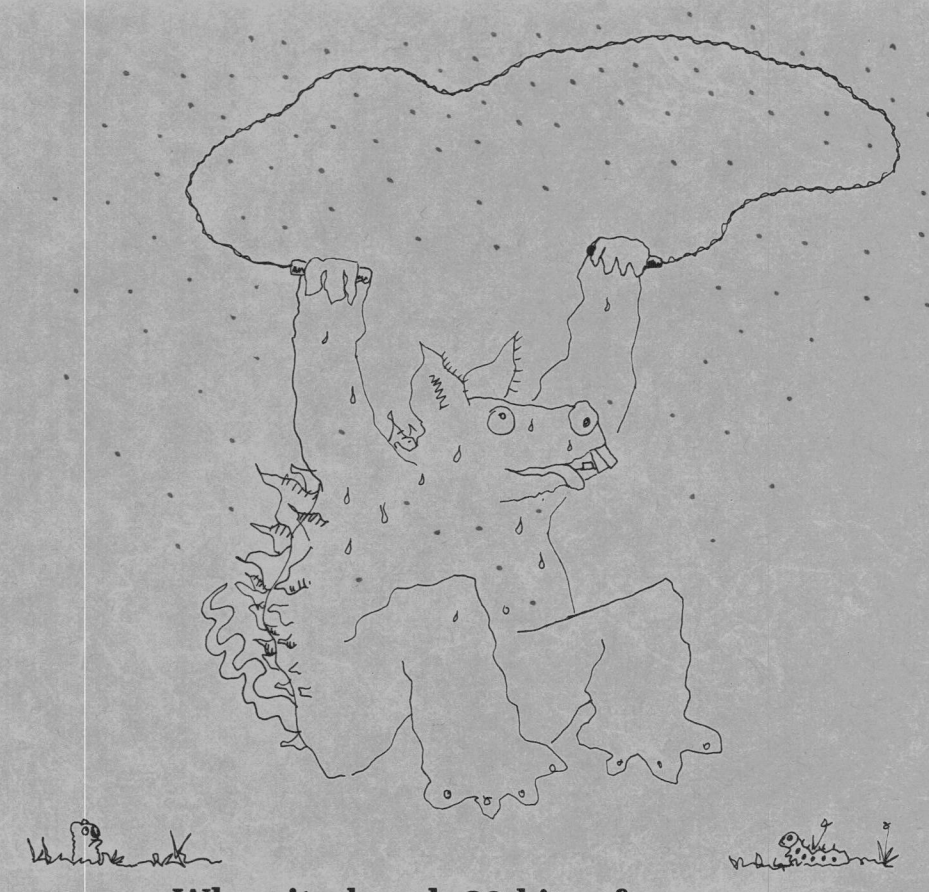

When it played, 90 bits of sun energy changed to heat and up and away it went.

10 bits of sun energy stayed in the spiny plant eater.

A sharp clawed meat eater came and ate the spiny plant eater.

It got the 10 bits of sun energy.

When it played, 9 bits of sun energy changed to heat and away it went.

How many bits stayed to help the sharp clawed meat eater grow?

Just one little bit!

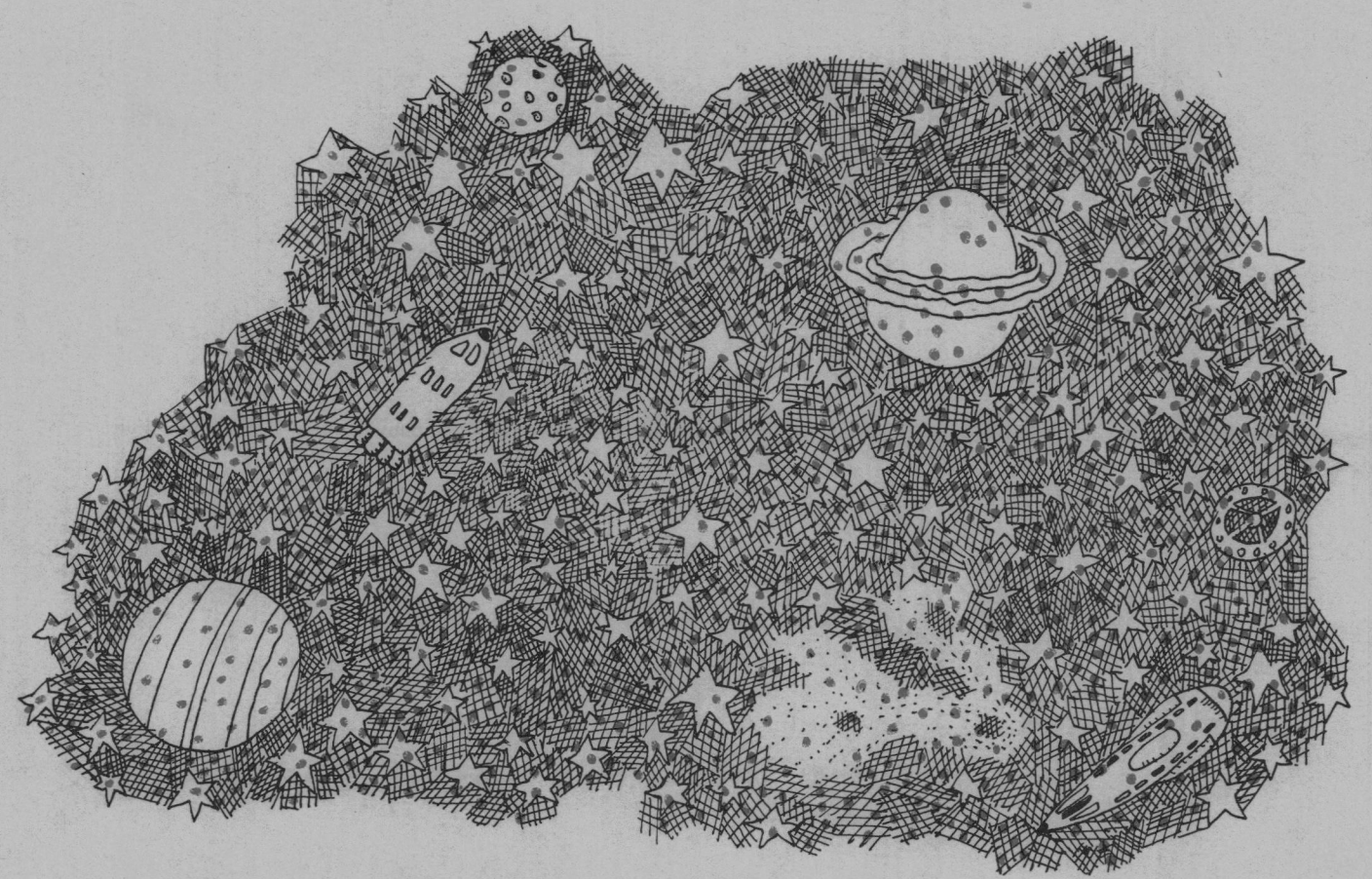

The other 999 bits were now bits of heat in outer space.

Every time energy is transferred, some changes into heat.

ENERGY RESOURCES

Have you ever heard of energy resources?   **No. What are energy resources?**

Energy resources are things that contain lots of energy.

Is the sun an energy resource? **The sun is our most important energy resource.**

The sun keeps us warm and gives us light.

Without the sun we would not have any plants.

Without plants there would be no food!

Without food there would be no energy for our bodies.

Without the sun there would be no other energy resources.

As a tree grows, it stores sun energy in its wood.

The bigger the tree gets, the more sun energy it contains.

When the tree is very old, it will still have the energy that it stored when it was young.

If you burn the tree, you will release the stored energy as light and heat.

Coal, oil and gas contain sun energy stored during the days of dinosaurs.

Uranium ore has sun energy stored from when the earth was made.

Wind contains energy from earth and water that have been heated by sun energy.

Water is carried up by sun energy. When it goes downhill, it contains sun energy.

All of our energy comes from the sun!

Efficiency

When we don't use energy resources efficiently we get waste.

What does efficiently mean?

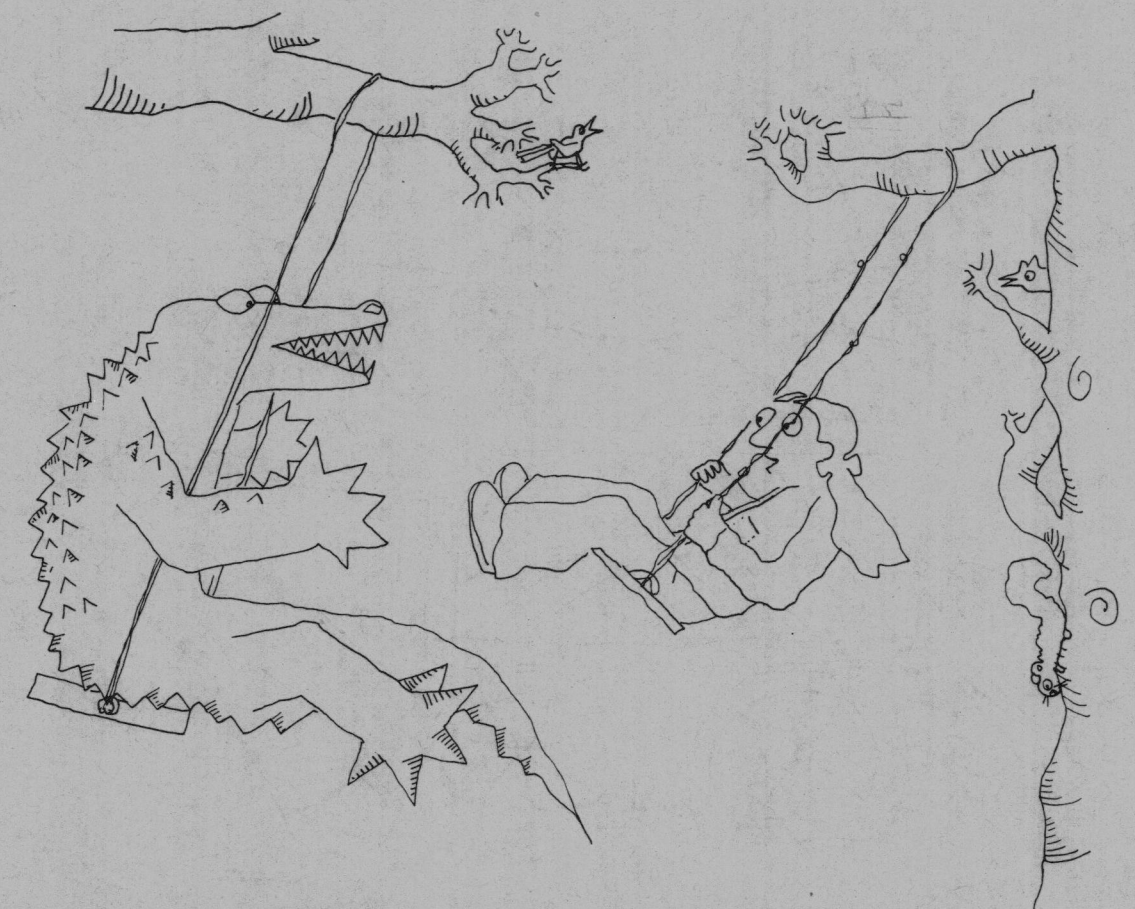

Efficiently means doing something with the least amount of energy.

Would it take less energy to pull a wagon with flat tires

or full tires?   Full tires!

Yes! Pulling a wagon with full tires is more efficient.

Which uses energy resources more efficiently, driving a mile

or walking a mile?   **I don't know.**

What makes more waste, walking or driving?   Driving, it makes smoke!

Driving is faster, but it uses more energy and makes more waste than walking.

So walking is more efficient!

Do you know what happens when you get too much waste from using energy resources?

No. What happens?

When you use coal, gas, oil or wood inefficiently, you get a lot of smoke.

Too much smoke can make you sick.

When we use uranium inefficiently, we get radioactive waste.

Radioactive waste makes living things sick too!

**When we use water energy inefficiently,
we cover too much land behind the dam with water.**

And more plants and animals lose their homes.

If we use our energy resources more efficiently,

the earth will be a healthier place for living things.

Book Energy

Is this the end?   **This is the end of the book, but not the end of the book's energy.**

Books are made from wood which contains stored sun energy.

If bugs eat the book, they will store some of the energy and the rest will turn to heat.

If you eat the bugs,

you might get enough energy to read another book!